B O D Y W O R K S

ears

Katherine Goode

BLACKBIRCH PRESS, INC.
WOODBRIDGE, CONNECTICUT

To Dr. Paul Goodman, with thanks

Published by Blackbirch Press, Inc.
260 Amity Road
Woodbridge, CT 06525

e-mail: staff@blackbirch.com
web site: www.blackbirch.com

Printed in Hong Kong

First published 1999 by
MACMILLAN EDUCATION AUSTRALIA PTY LTD
627 Chapel Street, South Yarra 3141

10 9 8 7 6 5 4 3 2 1

Photo Credits:
Cover photo: ©Dick McCabe
Page 16: A.N.T.; pages 14, 15: Graham Meadows; pages 4, 5, 16, 17, 19, 26: Great Southern Stock; pages 1, 10, 11, 20, 22, 23, 24, 25, 27, 28, 30: The Picture Source.

Library of Congress Cataloging-in-Publication Data
Goode, Katherine, 1949–
Ears / by Katherine Goode.
      p.   cm. — (Bodyworks)
   Includes index.
   Summary: Explains the functions of the different parts of the ear.
   ISBN 1-56711-496-2 (hardcover : alk. paper)
   1. Ear—Juvenile literature. [1. Ear.] I. Title.
QP461.G596   2000
612.8'5—dc21   00-008106
                                                            CIP

Contents

The ears

You use your ears to hear. Your ears can hear many different kinds of sound. They can hear the loud sound of a barking dog or the soft sound of a purring cat. Your ears also help you to keep your balance.

You depend on your ears to give you messages and warnings. They let you hear the noisy sounds of an ambulance siren or a fire engine.

Parts of the ear

Each of your ears has 3 parts: the outer ear, the middle ear, and the inner ear.

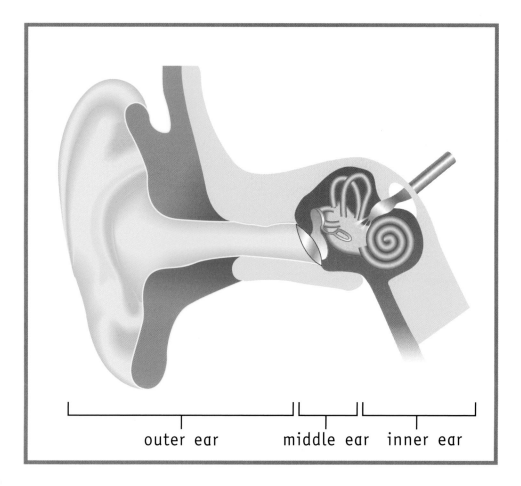

outer ear   middle ear inner ear

The outer ear

You can see the outer part of your ear. It is called the auricle. It is made up of skin, elastic **tissue**, and fat. The fatty tissue is in your earlobes. The opening of your ear is the beginning of your ear canal. Your eardrum separates your outer ear from your middle ear.

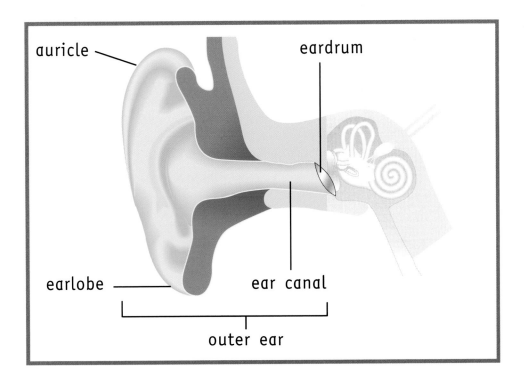

auricle

eardrum

earlobe

ear canal

outer ear

The middle ear

Your middle ear has 3 small bones. They are called the hammer, the anvil, and the stirrup. The 3 bones connect your eardrum to your inner ear.

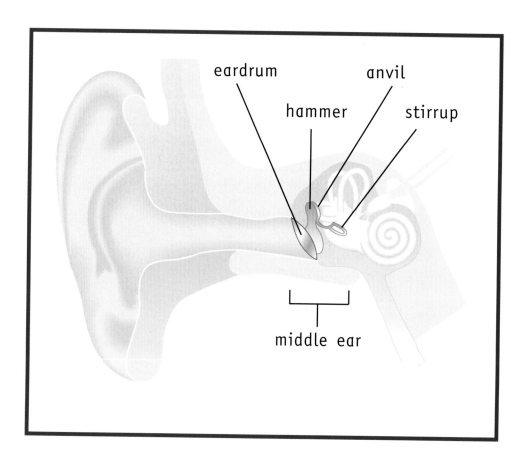

The inner ear

Your inner ear is filled with fluid. It is made up of the semicircular canals, the vestibule, and the cochlea. Sound waves travel in the fluid.

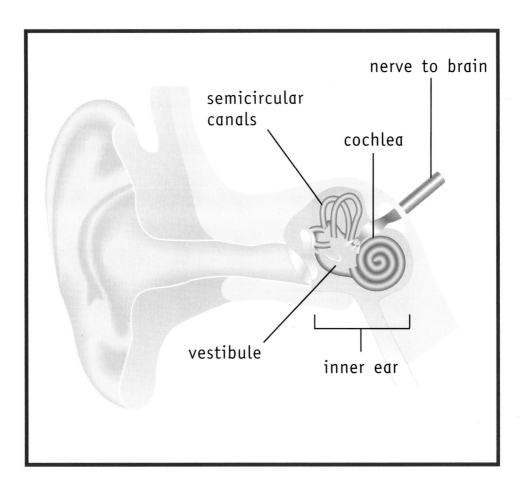

nerve to brain

semicircular canals

cochlea

vestibule

inner ear

How we hear

Your outer ear traps sound waves. The sound waves travel down the ear canal to your eardrum. Your eardrum starts to **vibrate**. The vibrations pass through your middle ear to the cochlea.

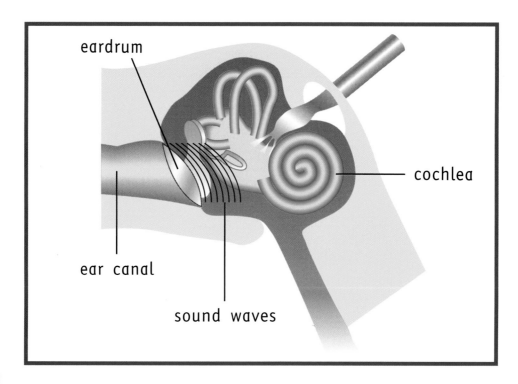

eardrum

cochlea

ear canal

sound waves

Your cochlea in your inner ear changes the sound waves into **nerve** signals. The nerve signals travel to the brain. Your brain then records the sounds so you can hear.

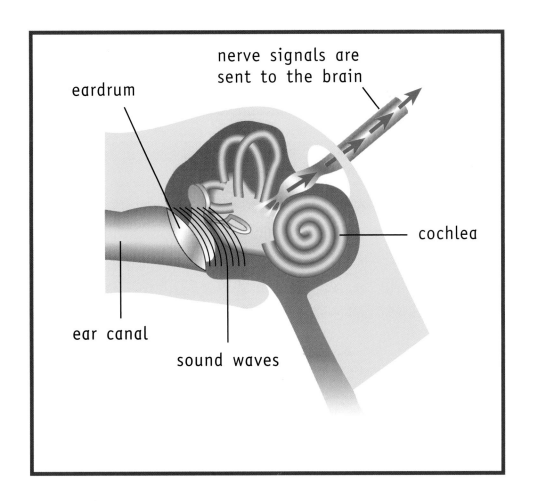

nerve signals are
sent to the brain

eardrum

cochlea

ear canal

sound waves

Sounds

Sounds can have either a high **pitch** or a low pitch. A whistle has a high pitch. Bass drums have a low pitch.

Sounds can be either soft or loud. Loud sounds can damage your ears. You can wear ear plugs or ear muffs to protect your ears from very loud noises.

The eustachian tubes

Eustachian tubes connect your middle ear to the inside of your nose. They keep air pressure the same on both sides of your eardrum. If air pressure changes too quickly (in an airplane), this may make your ears "pop."

The eustachian tubes are normally closed. They open when you chew, swallow, yawn, or blow your nose.

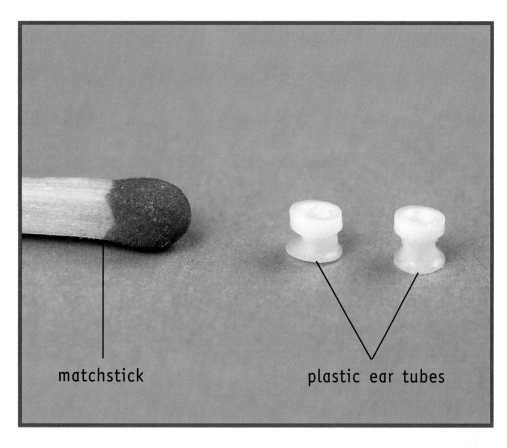

matchstick   plastic ear tubes

Ear tubes are smaller than the tip of a matchstick.

Sometimes an ear **infection** can block the eustachian tubes. The tubes fill up with fluid. Sometimes a doctor will put plastic ear tubes in the eardrum to help drain the fluid.

Balance

The semicircular canals in your inner ear help you to keep your balance. The canals are filled with fluid. When you move, the fluid moves. Tiny hairs in the canals sense the fluid and send balance messages to your brain.

If your semicircular canals become damaged,
they may send too few or too many messages
to your brain. This can make you feel dizzy or
sick to your stomach.

Animal ears

All mammals and birds use their ears to hear and to keep their balance. Insects do not have true ears. They have thin **membranes** on each of their legs that vibrate when sound waves strike them.

membrane

membrane

Frogs, snakes, and fish do not have outer ears. They have membranes that "hear" by feeling vibrations in the air, in water, or on the ground.

Most mammals have outer ears. Elephants can move their ears. They wave them like fans to cool themselves off in warm weather.

Bats use sounds in a special way. They make high-pitched sounds and then listen for an echo from nearby objects. The echo helps them to avoid objects when they fly.

Hearing problems

Sometimes head injuries or working in a noisy place can damage a person's hearing. Many people also lose some of their hearing as they get older.

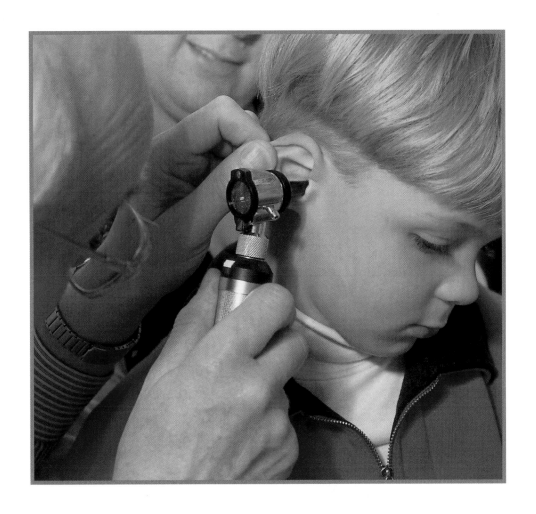

If you have trouble hearing, you may need to have an ear exam. The doctor will check the **earwax** in your ear and look at your eardrum.

Doctors can test your hearing. They use a
machine that records how well you can hear
low and high sounds. This machine also
records how loud a sound needs to be before
you can hear it.

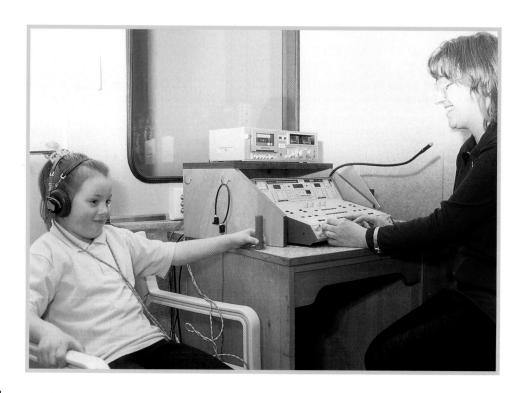

Hearing aids

A hearing aid can help with hearing problems. It makes sounds louder. It is small and uses batteries. A hearing aid can either be placed around the outer ear or put inside the ear canal.

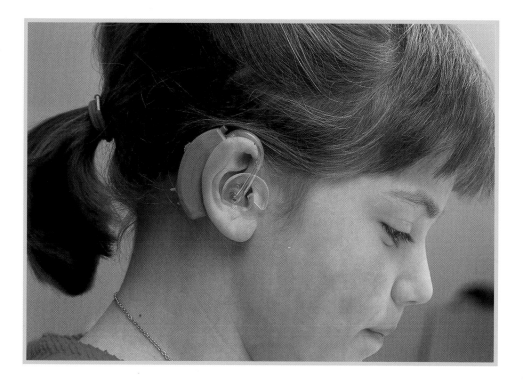

Deafness

Some people have little or no hearing. Many television programs now have captions for deaf people called "closed captions." A TV displays printed words, or subtitles, as the words are spoken.

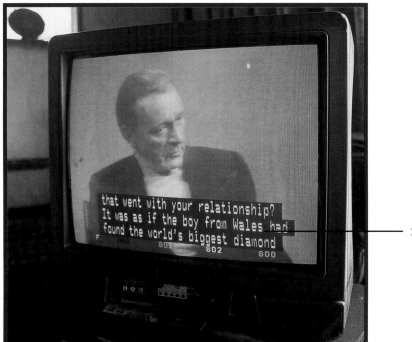

subtitles

A keyboard with a computer screen can help a deaf person "talk" on the telephone.

At home, deaf people can use other special ways to "hear." Some listening devices have flashing lights. The lights flash when the telephone or doorbell rings. Guide dogs can also be trained to hear important sounds for deaf people.

Sign language

Some deaf people learn sign language to communicate. This language is made up of hand and body movements and different facial expressions.

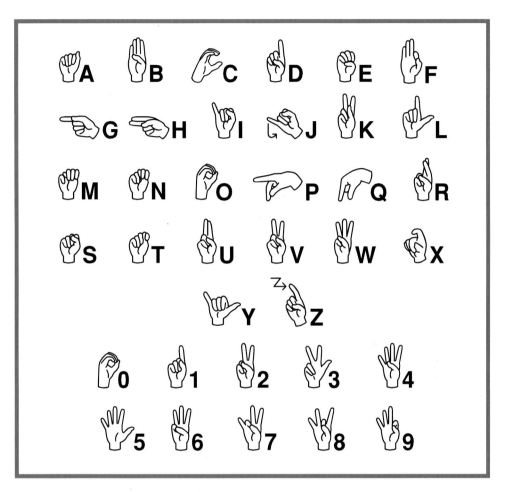

This is the American Sign Language alphabet.

In America, the sign language is called American Sign Language (ASL). ASL uses finger signs to spell words.

Ear care

It is important to take good care of your ears. You should clean your outer ears with soap and water. You should dry them off after you take a shower or go swimming. You should never put anything inside your ears.

Glossary

earwax   a sticky substance in the ear canal that traps dust

infection   a disease often caused by germs

membranes   thin pieces of tissue

nerves   the cells that carry signals to the brain that enable us to feel, see, hear, and taste

pitch   the way a sound strikes the ear, as high or low

tissue   the matter that living things are made of

vibrate   to move quickly up and down or back and forth

Index

DATE			